Making Sounds

Editorial planning: Serpentine Editorial
Scientific consultant: Dr. J.J.M. Rowe

Designed by The R & B Partnership
Illustrator: David Anstey
Photographer: Peter Millard

Additional photographs:
Chris Fairclough Colour Library 15, 18;
ZEFA 27; The Hutchison Library 30 (top);
Eye Ubiquitous 30 (bottom);
Martin Wendler/NHPA 31.

Library of Congress Cataloging-in-Publication Data

Rowe, Julian.
     Making sounds / by Julian Rowe and Molly Perham.
        p.   cm. — (First science)
     Includes index.
     Summary: Describes in simple words different sounds, how they are made, and
how they travel.
        ISBN 0-516-08136-5
        1. Sound—Experiments—Juvenile literature. 2. Sound-waves—Experiments—
Juvenile literature. [1. Sound—Experiments. 2. Experiments.]
     I. Perham, Molly. II. Title. III. Series: First science (Chicago, Ill.)
     QC225.5.R69 1993
     534'.078—dc20   93-13738
                                                                              CIP
                                                                               AC

1993 Childrens Press® Edition
© 1993 Watts Books, London
1 2 3 4 5 6 7 8 9 10 R 02 01 00 99 98 97 96 95 94 93

First Science

Making Sounds

Julian Rowe
and Molly Perham

CHILDRENS PRESS®
CHICAGO

Contents

 SAFETY WARNING

Activities marked with this symbol require the presence and
help of an adult. Plastic should always be used instead of glass.

Listening

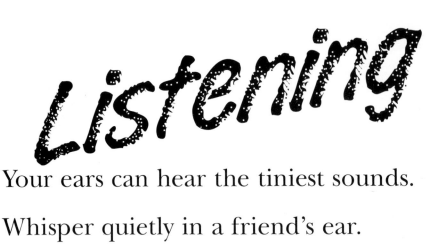

Your ears can hear the tiniest sounds.

Whisper quietly in a friend's ear.
Every word can be heard
if you cup your hand.

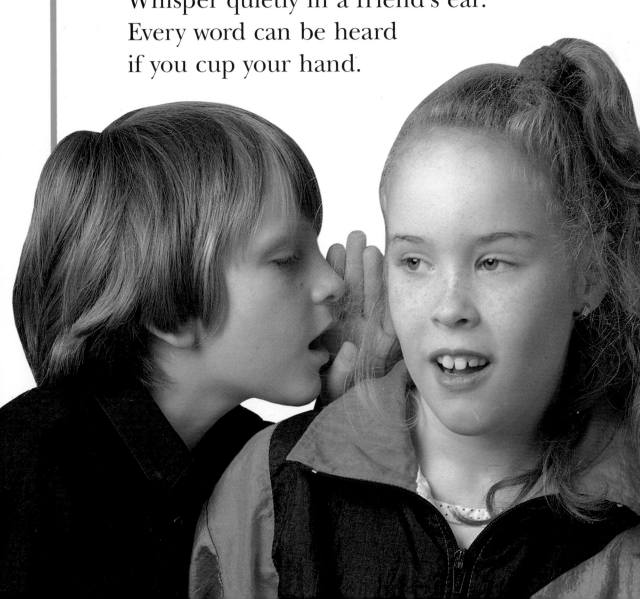

If it is very quiet,
you can hear

a
pin
drop.

It helps if you drop the
pin onto a metal tray!
Why do you think this works better?

Clashing cymbals together makes a lot of
noise. You can hear cymbals playing in a
band from far away. They are very loud.

Hearing sounds

A megaphone helps the sound of your voice reach a long distance away. Most of the sound is pointed in the same direction instead of spreading out in all directions. Pointing all the sound in one direction makes it louder.

Make a megaphone

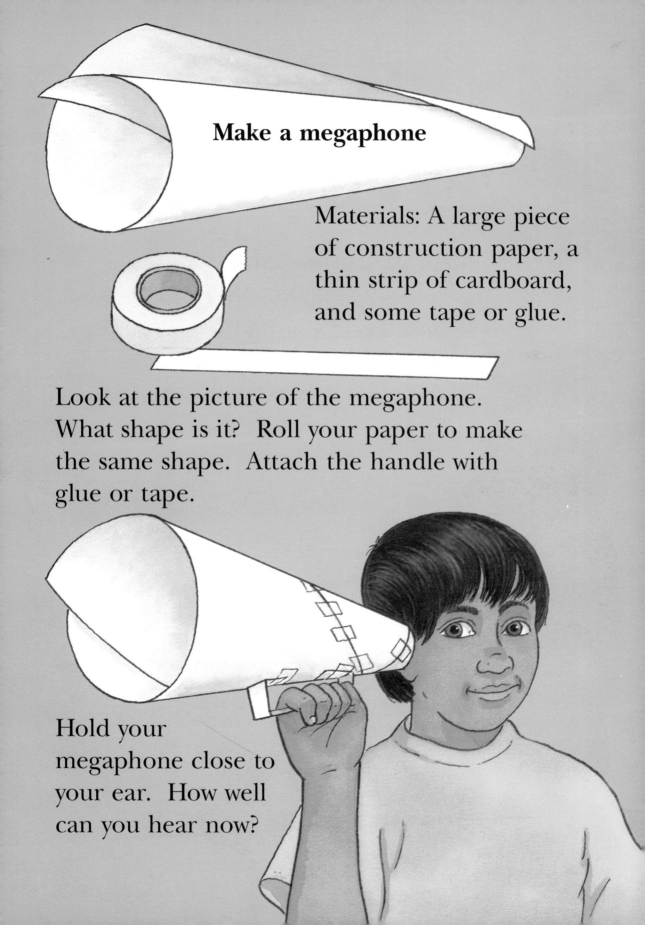

Materials: A large piece of construction paper, a thin strip of cardboard, and some tape or glue.

Look at the picture of the megaphone. What shape is it? Roll your paper to make the same shape. Attach the handle with glue or tape.

Hold your megaphone close to your ear. How well can you hear now?

Noise

Sometimes we wish we did not hear so
clearly. Noises are loud sounds we do not
want to hear. Very loud noise can damage
your ears. Putting your hands over
your ears makes the noise softer.
People who work in noisy places
often wear ear protectors.

This alarm clock has a very loud tick.
Wrapping a wool sweater around the
clock stops some of the sound waves
from escaping.

What do you think it sounds like now?

Traveling sounds

A sound that comes from a long way off takes some time to reach us. We can see something happen before we hear it.

This girl sees the boy banging the cymbals before she hears the clash.

Sound travels through other materials
as well as through air. It travels through
wood. In this picture a watch is taped
onto one side of a door. A girl is
standing close to the door. Do you
think she can hear the watch ticking?

Making a sound

A sound is made by tiny, fast movements of the air. These pass into your ear and make your eardrum vibrate. Messages about the vibrations go to your brain, and you hear a sound.

When you clap your hands, the air around your hands vibrates and forms waves.

Drop a pebble in some water.

See how the ripples or waves travel
outward in larger and larger circles. The
pebble has stirred up the water around it
and made the ripples. These ripples
spread out like sound waves.

A sound is waves of air. You can hear a
sound but you cannot see it.

Speaking

Can you feel a sound? Put your fingers on your throat and say something.

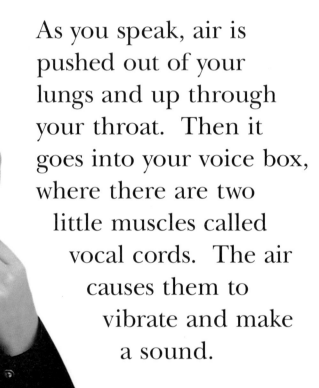

As you speak, air is pushed out of your lungs and up through your throat. Then it goes into your voice box, where there are two little muscles called vocal cords. The air causes them to vibrate and make a sound.

You can feel these vibrations with your fingers.

Blow up a balloon and stretch the neck
sideways as you let out the air. As you stretch
the neck in and out, the sound will change.
Your vocal cords work in the same way.

Musical sounds

A musical instrument produces a sound by making the air around it vibrate.

The strings of stringed instruments make the air vibrate when they are plucked or played with a bow.

Wind instruments work when you blow on the column of air inside them.

Percussion instruments have a tight piece of skin or plastic, or a piece of metal or wood. These make the air vibrate when you bang, scrape, or shake them.

How do these instruments make the air
vibrate to make a sound?

Musical strings

This guitar player plucks the strings to make music. When a string is plucked, its vibrations cause sound waves in the air. As these waves reach our ears we hear a note.

The player makes high and low notes by pressing strings with the fingers of his left hand.

Make a guitar

Materials: Two large rubber bands, two pencils, and a book. Stretch the rubber bands around the book. Push the pencils under the rubber bands. Press down one of the strings with your finger to change the length of the string that you pluck.

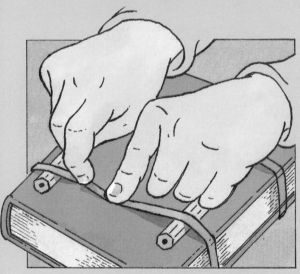

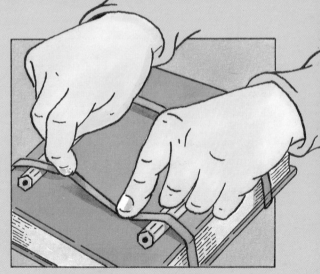

Plucking a short string makes a high note.

Plucking a long string makes a low note.

The rubber bands are like the strings of a guitar.

Musical pipes

The recorder player blows the air inside the pipe to make music. She moves her fingers on and off the holes to produce different notes. When a hole is open near the top of the recorder, some of the air in the pipe escapes. When there is less air it vibrates quickly and produces a high note.

Make a bottle organ

Materials: Six plastic bottles that are the same size and shape. Stand the bottles in a line and pour different amounts of water into each one. Blow across the tops of the bottles. Each one makes a different note.

Which one makes the highest note?

Which one makes the lowest note?

Musical drums

A drum has a piece of thin material called a drumhead stretched across the top. When you bang the drumhead, it vibrates and makes sound waves in the air. This drummer is turning a screw to make the drumhead tighter.

A tight drumhead vibrates faster and produces a high note. When it is looser, it vibrates more slowly and produces a low note.

Materials: A hollow container, plastic wrap, tape or a strong rubber band, and a wooden spoon.

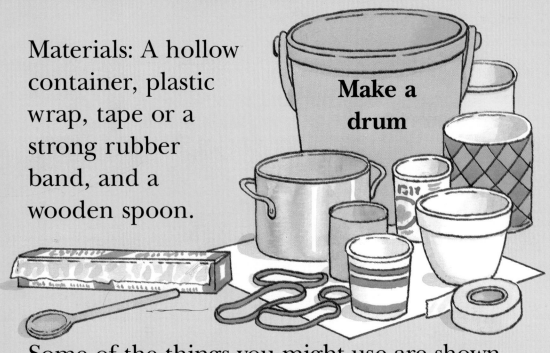

Make a drum

Some of the things you might use are shown below. Stretch the plastic wrap tightly over the container to make the drumhead. Tape down the edges firmly, or use the rubber band.

Use the spoon for a drumstick.

Warning sounds

Loud sounds can be useful because they warn us of danger.

A bicycle horn warns people to keep out of the way.

When it is very foggy at sea the
lighthouse uses its foghorn to warn
ships that land is near.

Can you think of some other warning sounds?

Useful sounds

A whistle can be a warning sound. During a soccer game, the referee blows a whistle to warn players that they are doing something wrong. The whistle also gives information about the time and the rules of the game.

The everyday
sounds around us
give us all kinds of
information. The
ringing of an alarm
clock tells us when
it is time to get up.

When the telephone
rings we know that
someone wants to
speak to us.
A telephone allows
us to speak and
listen to people
a long way off.

Two-way radios help
firefighters and
police officers
organize help and
rescue people
quickly.

Think about... sounds

This boy cannot hear. He is deaf. But he can speak to other people using a sign language.

This worker must protect his ears. The noise of the road drill is very loud. Without the ear protectors, he would become deaf.

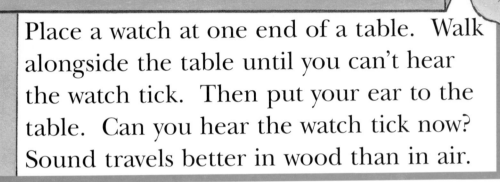

Place a watch at one end of a table. Walk alongside the table until you can't hear the watch tick. Then put your ear to the table. Can you hear the watch tick now? Sound travels better in wood than in air.

The fennec fox has huge ears. It uses them to hear the tiny sounds made by the small animals it hunts. What other animals have large ears?

INDEX